Don't Dig for Water Under the Outhouse

and Other Cowboy Commandments

TEXAS BIX BENDER

Illustrations by

L. BARK'KARIE

GIBBS·SMITH
P
PUBLISHER

SALT LAKE CITY

First Edition
05 04 03 02 01 00   6 5 4 3 2 1

Published by
Gibbs Smith, Publisher
P.O. Box 667
Layton, Utah 84041

Web site: www.gibbs-smith.com
Orders: (800) 748-5439

Library of Congress Cataloging-in-Publication Data

Bender, Texas Bix, 1949–
Don't dig for water under the outhouse and other cowboy
commandments / by Texas Bix Bender.
    p. cm.
ISBN 0-87905-977-X
1. Conduct of life—Humor. 2. Cowboys—Humor.
3. Maxims. I. Title.

PN6231.C6142 B46 2000
818'.5402—dc21
00-022224

Don't let the sun catch you in bed.

IF IT AIN'T RIGHT,
DON'T DO IT.

IF THE BOOTS FIT,
KEEP GETTING 'EM
RESOLED.

WHAT'S WANTED
ISN'T ALWAYS
WHAT'S NEEDED.

DON'T LET YOUR YEARNINGS GET AHEAD OF YOUR EARNINGS.

IF YOU VALUE IT, TAKE
CARE OF IT.

NEVER WEAR OUT
YOUR HORSE.

SPREAD HAPPINESS
WHERE YOU GO,
NOT WHEN.

IF YOU DON'T FEEL
LIKE SMILING, GIVE IT
A SHOT ANYWAY. IT'LL
HELP THE GENERAL
SCHEME OF THINGS.

Keep your moccasins greased.

IF THE BOOT FITS,
MAKE SURE THERE'S
TWO OF 'EM.

FOR BETTER
OR FOR WORSE
MEANS
FOR GOOD.

FALL IN LOVE
ONLY WHEN YOU
CAN'T HELP IT.

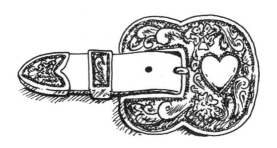

DON'T LOOK AT
THINGS FOR WHAT
THEY'RE NOT,
LOOK AT THEM FOR
WHAT THEY ARE.

THE SIDE OF LIFE YOU
SEE IS THE SIDE OF
LIFE YOU SHOW.

NEVER CUSS
SOMEBODY ELSE'S DOG
OR ABUSE YOUR OWN.

CONTROL YOUR
TEMPER BEFORE YOU
TRY TO CONTROL
A HORSE.

NEVER TAKE
UNFAIR ADVANTAGE.

DON'T SPUR A HORSE WHEN HE'S SWIMMING.

NEVER MISS
A GOOD CHANCE
TO SHUT UP.

TO KNOW
THE TRUTH,
SPEAK THE TRUTH.

IF IT'S NONE
OF YOUR BUSINESS,
STAY OUT OF IT.

If it ain't botherin' you, leave it alone.

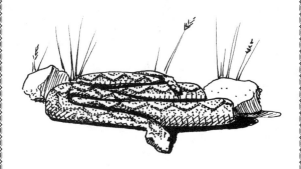

NEVER TAKE DOWN
ANOTHER MAN'S
FENCE.

Always sink corner fence posts twice as deep.

NEVER PICK A FIGHT
WITH A PORCUPINE.

Don't forget that there are always consequences.

DON'T BE
TOO SOON AND
DON'T BE TOO
SELDOM.

NEVER
LOSE YOUR WAY
HOME.

A LOT OF GETTING BY
IS GOTTEN BY
DOING THINGS
YOU'D RATHER NOT DO.

WHEN YOU GET BUCKED OFF, GET BACK ON.

FIND THE PROBLEM
BEFORE YOU FIND
THE SOLUTION.

KEEP ONLY FIVE BEANS
IN THE WHEEL AND
KEEP THE HAMMER
DOWN ON THE
EMPTY CHAMBER.

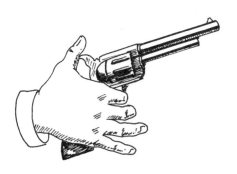

TRY TO GET YOUR WIFE
A JOB IN TOWN.

CHERISH WOMEN, HORSES, WATER, AND GRASS.

SKIN YOUR OWN DEER.

DO NOT
TOLERATE
WEAK COFFEE.

NEVER DRIVE
BLACK CATTLE
IN THE DARK.

NEVER RIDE
A SORE-BACKED HORSE.

IF IT BREAKS,
FIX IT.

Never cut
what you can untie.

IF YOU CAN
DO IT YOURSELF,
DON'T ASK FOR HELP.

BE A GOOD
WORKER.

NEVER DO ANYTHING
THAT WILL MAKE YOU
AFRAID TO LOOK
YOURSELF IN THE EYE.

STAND UP STRAIGHT
AND GIVE FOLKS
SOMETHING TO
LOOK AT.

IF YOU MAKE A MESS,
CLEAN IT UP.

A CLEAN SADDLE BLANKET IS MORE IMPORTANT THAN CLEAN SHEETS.

WHEN EXPERIENCE
TALKS, LET YOUR
EARS HANG DOWN
AND LISTEN.

Things
don't change
as much as you do.

DEAD DUCKS
DON'T NEED KILLING.

THE ONLY
GOOD REASON TO
RIDE A BULL IS TO
MEET A NURSE.

IF YOU DON'T KNOW
HOW TO RUN IT,
LEAVE IT ALONE.

DON'T GET YOUR
SPURS TANGLED.

TALK LESS
AND
SAY MORE.

NEVER
BETRAY A TRUST.

WHEN YOU TAKE
A HERD TO WATER,
TAKE 'EM SLOW
AND SPREAD 'EM OUT
UPSTREAM.

NEVER HURRY
WEAK STOCK.

KEEP YOUR WORDS
OUT OF THE
TALL GRASS.

DON'T TALK DOWN
TO ANYONE, EVEN IF
IT MEANS GETTIN' OFF
YOUR HORSE.

MAKE APOLOGIES
NOT EXCUSES.

HOLD YOUR PIECE
UNTIL YOU'RE SURE
YOU KNOW WHAT
YOU'RE TALKIN' ABOUT.

DON'T GET EVEN—
GET OVER IT.

DON'T WASTE
GOOD MONEY
ON CHEAP BOOTS.

YOUR VALUE GOES
UP AND DOWN
EVERY DAY DEPENDING
ON HOW YOU
TREAT OTHER FOLKS.

BE KIND
TO ANIMALS.

WATER AND TRUTH
ARE FRESHEST
AT THEIR SOURCE.

WATER AND SOAP
DON'T COST MUCH;
STAY CLEAN.

IF YOU START IT,
STOP IT.

IF YOU OPEN IT,
CLOSE IT.

IT'S NOT SO MUCH
WHAT YOU
CALL YOURSELF
THAT MATTERS,
IT'S WHAT YOU
CALL OTHERS.

TAKE AS GOOD A CARE
OF YOUR HORSE AS
YOU DO YOURSELF.

DON'T LOOK
FOR COURAGE
IN A BOTTLE.

DON'T GO IN
IF YOU DON'T KNOW
THE WAY OUT.

NEVER WORK
FOR A MAN
WITH ELECTRICITY
IN HIS BARN.
YOU'LL BE UP
ALL NIGHT.

IF YOU
TOSS YOUR BEDROLL
IN THE WAGON,
RIDE FOR THE BRAND.

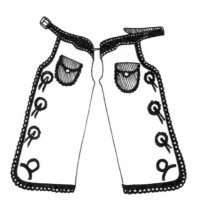

SAY WHAT YOU
LIKE TO HEAR.

GOOD MANNERS GO
A LONG WAY TOWARDS
MAKING ANYBODY
MORE ATTRACTIVE.

When you're heading
down a long road
with a heavy load,
don't look back, and
don't look too far
ahead, just keep
taking it a step at
a time and you'll
get there.

HELP WHAT YOU CAN;
ENDURE WHAT YOU CAN'T.

SUSPICION
AIN'T PROOF.

DON'T LEAVE SPUR MARKS ON A HORSE.

BRACE YOUR BACKBONE
AND FORGET YOUR
WISHBONE.

IF YOU CLIMB IN THE
SADDLE, BE READY
FOR THE RIDE.

DON'T BUILD
THE GATE
UNTIL YOU'VE BUILT
THE CORRAL.

DO THINGS
WHEN YOU
FIRST KNOW
THEY NEED DOIN'.

WEIGH YOUR WORDS, DON'T COUNT 'EM.

No whining.

WORK HARD
TO LEAVE A BIG HOLE
WHEN YOU DIE.

DON'T PUT YOUR RELIGION IN YOUR WIFE'S NAME.

TAKE YOUR "TAKE
HOME PAY" HOME.

SET THE PACE BY
THE DISTANCE.

PUT OFF
'TIL TOMORROW
WHAT YOU
SHOULDN'T BE
DOING ANYWAY.

RIDE WITH
YOUR HEAD,
NOT YOUR BUTT.

Always cut
the cards.

A FULL HOUSE
DIVIDED DON'T
WIN ANY POTS.

DON'T ARGUE JUST
FOR THE HELL OF IT.

TAKE THINGS BY THE SMOOTH HANDLE.

WHEN SOMEBODY
DOES YOU A FAVOR,
REMEMBER IT.
WHEN YOU DO A
FAVOR, FORGET IT.

FRIENDS LAST LONGER
THE LESS THEY
ARE USED.

DON'T DO NOTHIN'
TOO MUCH.

A COW OUTFIT'S
NEVER ANY BETTER
THAN ITS HORSES.

NO POOTS AROUND
THE CAMPFIRE.

NEVER WALK BEHIND
A STRANGE HORSE.

IF YOU SAY IT,
MEAN IT.

Don't pack
hardware for bluff
or ballast.

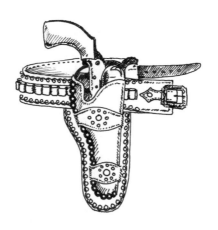

DON'T WORRY A GOOD
THING TOO HARD.

DON'T PLAY WITH
THE CAT IF
YOU'RE THE MOUSE.

THINK TWICE BEFORE
YOU PUT YOUR
TWO CENTS IN.
MOST TIMES
YOU WON'T HAVE TO
SPEND A PENNY.

JUDGE A MAN BY WHAT HE DOES, NOT WHAT HE WEARS.

TAKE PLEASURE IN YOUR BUSINESS.

HONOR YOUR FATHER AND YOUR MOTHER.

DON'T BORROW
IF YOU CAN BUY.

DON'T DESIRE WHAT
YOU CAN'T ACQUIRE.

DO IT TODAY.
TOMORROW IS
PROMISED TO
NO ONE.

START SOONER, TRAVEL FASTER, ARRIVE BEFORE YOU'RE EXPECTED.

KEEP COOL,
BUT DON'T FREEZE.

DON'T APPROACH
BULLS FROM THE
FRONT OR HORSES
FROM THE REAR.

THE LOSER
IN A FIGHT
AIN'T NECESSARILY
WRONG.

Keep your guts in line with your gumption.

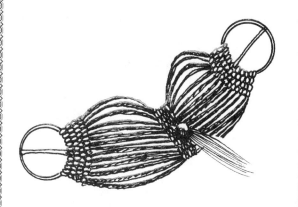

SING,
DON'T CRY.

NEVER MISS
A CHANCE TO DANCE.

ACT RIGHT,
BEHAVE YOURSELF,
DO YOUR JOB, AND
THINGS WILL TURN
OUT ALL RIGHT.

TAKE CARE OF YOUR
KNEES; YOU'RE GOING
TO NEED THEM ALL
YOUR LIFE.

DON'T WAIT 'TIL
THE GATE'S CLOSING
TO GET OUTTA
THE CORRAL.

PUT AWAY YOUR HORSE
BEFORE YOU PUT AWAY
YOUR DINNER.

DO YOUR BEST,
THAT'S ALL.